Thirst & Surfeit

Thirst & Surfeit

Elizabeth Robinson

Threadsuns 2023
High Point, North Carolina

Published by Threadsuns, High Point, NC 27268

EDITORIAL
Nicole Prince
Katie Craun

DESIGN
Julianne Kendrick
Alexander Rucker

MARKETING
Courtney Collar
Erica Johnson

First Edition
27 26 25 24 23 1 2 3 4 5

ISBN 978-1-7346911-4-6

LIBRARY OF CONGRESS CONTROL NUMBER: 2023934538

Thirst & Surfeit is set in Athelas, with Century Schoolbook and Century Gothic displays.

Acknowledgments

Many thanks to the editors of the following publications for bringing my work into print: *Bombay Gin, Chicago Quarterly Review, Colorado Review, Denver Quarterly, Cutbank, For Immediate Release, Interim, Pulchritudinous Review, Radical Society, St. Elizabeth Street,* and *Third Bed.*

Additional thanks to editors at High5 Press for publishing a chapbook length version of *Thirst or Surfeit* and the Lefthand Series for publishing the chapbook *The War of the End of the World.* I am indebted to editors Cole Swensen and David St. John for including poems in this manuscript in the Norton Anthology, *American Hybrid.*

The poems in "The Canudos Rebellion" speak to a peasant rebellion in the backlands of Bahia, Brazil. It was led by an itinerant mystic and preacher, Antonio Conselheiro. The uprising was crushed by the Brazilian Army in 1897 at which time they are estimated to have killed 15,000 people. My initial awareness of the massacre resulted from reading Mario Vargas Llosa's *The War of the End of the World.*

Contents

Thirst & Surfeit

THE BOG TRAVERSE

1200-600 B.C.E.

Tollund Man

A name finds itself in a bog, filtered. And then it bears ridicule in relation to the ridiculous. What is it upon which you rest but a skin made, literally, into leather?

Weight has a purifying character. Pelt made metal. Once, your face was a fingerprint: not made for purposes of identification, but for assertion. Time's serenity borrows its voice from sphagnum, old photos, rubberized bones. A reticule of fuel.

The Windeby Girl

Death is not death but a blindfold. Rock in the crook of your arm. Even in war, when cotton bandages were in short supply, they made substitutions, just as you did. The woolen headband shifts from your bare head and covers your eyes. Stanched with water, the despite of flows. Girl, girl, they called you from time immemorial when you might have swallowed your sexual organs. This burnished skin peeled back from your ribcage to reveal your hips. What grows shallow derives from itself.

Yde

Fear has necessary relation to fact, this red-haired body. Now you run from those brick-like portions you've excavated as merely domestic goods. Fear pegged down as a compass tells you which way to run. Away. Not to say you were only a child. Here is a disability of relation. Form preserved eats the DNA entire. One thought the covering layer was the devil and the thing unearthed was fear. Those wisps of hair, not like a face beneath. One thought her slanted spine had a finger's indication.

"I have great pleasure in sending you the customary, annual bog body. . ."

Now I should be stepping distant from you, credulous grace. Borremose, we are old lovers in the gaping noose of you. Your semen hemmed in resorbs to peat and deerskin. Without hands, it's the grasp of your face that swallows; there is no further clenching I might be able to believe.

The next year, another was uncovered in the same bog. And in 1948, still a third body was discovered there. Incubated in thirst or surfeit. Slowly the stride recesses from the place; and resumes. Its Swabian knot.

Surfaced

I think of the basic quality of infidelity as a perch from which to view. This is a thing a mummy would not know, so long as we discriminate mummies from skeletons. The cause of death, seen from this distance, half immured: the origin of science. No less than the one who betrayed her head as it struggled above the water's line.

Meenybradden Woman

Your conscience has a face, blurred and fibrous. There a hand unfurls, from below expression, to brush the hair back from the brow. Here stood a good wife and here stood her cottage. And here came the angry cauldron to smear her with preservative, a spoon surrounded with itself. And here I came, from out of your cape, by a 500 years' margin. It is as you wish: by right to be disinterred and by virtue to be cast back. Tendered to the true face and disclosed.

Wiedergånger

Where offerings were made.

Some such were insured never to walk there again. Like a scoliosis that affected her gait, that lifted the stain from around her wicket. That's the solicitude of the maze, sieved with quicksand. The riddles chime, gong, bell, flute. So the wand lifted inhales the banner.

No one. And such damage inflicted in no other ware.

HOVENWEEP

1200-1300 C.E.

You are not now what you were meant to be. And this is why mirages are without irony.

So hurry: the precipate falls hard onto forgetful dirt. The external, like rain, jars you.

There are stretches of miles, of the unexpected; they menace and recant. You prefer that the haste drop you off like a passenger, into tedium. You are in brambles that annoy but do not scratch.

A cartoonish body waits outside yours, whistling and smirking.

The precipitous

falls sodden-to-itself, to shoulders like yours, piggyback.
Hard. Finally, hurtful: this patience.
The trees named for Joshua pick up their arms, plainly out of obedience.

The ornamentation on the desert falls away, ashamed. Animals
pare the infrared light
as light
made invisible to them.

Why would any flock leave

these blemishes—

here—

whereas the light will shrug, give admittance, lay reddened sod carpet
over the barrier, a cattle guard

when single phrases lining the grammar are stilted, self-conscious.

    The group which makes them
    drifts

across a site so difficult to disparage.

Light untied and undone.

The herd, and all excess rubbed out.

Hackberry cancels out juniper   Travel approximately forty-five miles on a road that is variably paved—

There was a testimonial painted on tin, regarding his journey,
traversed entirely
on his knees.

As though the humble man could crawl the entire way, but end up only here.

And still mark his disappointment as affirmation.

This is what's accomplished
in the

creek, water rotting away
the rock.

Your compass: obliges you to take him out briefly to the night, look up, and him crawling and panting in the dark.

You, at the base looking flat, see north. See towers.   It may take a long time.

We look down, straight down, on you from above. It was forty five minutes of flight over an unpaved road

and we saw that ruined honeycomb

as we were masons

who knew better. The weathertight world

and all that's inclement cast aside: affirmation for assertion.

Tower is a term of endearment. That you not disgrace your family by insisting they must be pilgrims with you. The names of those places.

And then those who are looking for the structure of honey go in your stead. Fallen rocks, and knees curved. The map consults upward to sweetness, its supplication, darkly sticky.

Aneth, Cortez, Blanding. Aneth and Cortez. Aneth. Aneth and Blanding. Aneth.

Turkey pens   Merriem's shrew

kangaroo rat   nutcracker   oriole   Brewer's blackbird   The artifacts

have pulses.

"I'm hungry" she says, incessantly. "I'm drinky," like a dialect

whose house sparrow and finch
grab at names which list their desire.

Won't you come in? Would you like something to drink? Can I make you a cup

of tea?   Guidebook to absent species

Merriem's shrew is redundant with want.

The prophetic. Here is the house

that no one built, gray-topped, linty, from a list of the fallen-in. Some evidence
circa 1974, and again, 1976

that causeways also consumed the site, drank this down. They fell down. Horned

Ash-throated   Vertebrates all. So the Silky Pocket Mouse defined just that, to the
last,

its silky pocket. And then they all, marvelously, disappeared.

Ah, now the face got washed away, acequia. Frontispiece or channel,

it was called "And." The monks, the brothers, all of us drank strong

coffee thickened with sugar. We studied the face. Collision with, that is.

The frontispiece. A building

inclined to melt.

Here was a channel by the name of "And" who was filled

quickly by a fierce cohort of poplars, shaking intensely. Then they went

away. And no one knows what became of this face, an off-hand loss,

like a book gone, half-way through the reading of it. The brothers.

The gouge in the flatness of things. And
swept through with kinship.

The essence of nature is to be always borrowing. The wing falls from the bird
mid-flight

and then is affixed elsewhere. Winged stones, winged weeds, and so forth. They jitter around like small dolls. The wind falls off the wing

in the semi-deliberate world. Dolls fall into a tableau. Twigs or flecks of dead skin.

Little angular dolls flop over, overlapping, making a corral
where there was once a corral. The essence of falling is repetition or overlap.

Summer is the most dilapidated season, most likely to stumble from overhead.

Most likely, these shabby playthings are ancient. Herding wild creatures into domesticity. A little spit will glue a leaf onto the doll's back, winglike.

But no saliva in a place devoid of mouths.

Toys, they lack their own volition, and for that, they are made to lie down and cover up the tools.

"The shadows walk on sunlight in the air" so said

a child, yellow-headed in the contrast he explicates. Remember to go

to the market, tomorrow, to retrieve what you left there. Go late, when it's sure
to be reachable, findable. The child will be gone. The fruit, the merchandise

all fine, but without any color. Just the canopy's flap. The father, who looks on.
You find yourself on the curb, grinding something down with your heel. Butt or pig-
ment, or a gesture that signifies defiance. This you throw over commerce

to imbue, again, with color, your lost holding. You are the historian.

And the color and gesture are genuine, but not the heel. Here's the child, he seems
to have disappeared from the woods, come back. But this place is hardly wooded,

and even the marketplace is just a tent where itinerants sell soda and candy. They've left. Now the child puts on a silence; he's burlap and dune. A pretend forest leans sideways to expose wares. The practical opposing irrelevant sunlight. With what's inside. These shadow's rocklike containers.

The plan is sticky, and unwinds slowly from around rock, shrub. For convenience, it abandons its twine-shape and adopts legs and arms. Lies on its side.

Having a greater surface area speeds evaporation. Salt crystals
attract goats and sunlight.

This is not the plan of a parasite. Not a patch of mistletoe, no lichen caught on the rock's face. Slow unwinding of arms from the clutch of a self. Unhurried gait.

There are rituals for stickiness. Where no water is available for rinsing, we chew through barriers. Where the barriers waft off, we call the former people.

Now it is a gummy ball, bouncing in a rut. When it is caught, it will, in turn, entrap. Boredom has its own mission. Like the purpose of aridity, it preserves.

Here is someone to whom the plan clings as she passes through. The rock and shrub bow together, confiding.

Someone sits cross-legged before three piles. Tallow, flint, and a mound of unknown things. She twists cotton wicks in her hands.

Elsewhere: she digs recklessly, throwing up dirt in what was, archeologically, a garden. There is a fossil hand grasping a fossil shovel. All this becomes evident in the aftermath of flames and wind. She invokes play

and the mortar falls into heaps. The careful ruins of fruit. The tentative petrification of herbs. Overripe by millennia, the place smells of shit. Evidence preceding a fire.

Some one will come along and counter the smell with another finding. Buried communities are not concerned about weather's vicissitudes. The cistern dries out into a primitive lantern. She digs not to unearth herself, but to absorb light from the detritus. She clenches her tail with a set of facsimile teeth.

The ruined towers

Now where will I go, as I have completed the task put before me and I am about to sob from frustration.

Maybe thousands of people have put their feet in these same tracks, have been swaddled with fat, and shuddered. What appears to be an endless plain is really rent by deep, narrow canyons that run southwest toward

some more than a thousand

feet deep.

Seeps,
what you suck from for nourishment, at the trick of source. Do this in such a way as to make the narrowest mesa an errand from which to fall. This falling is part of the comic mask. The gibberish I've recited. Something dark and blue trickled from my mouth while a crippled man literally walked on air above the lines recited. The lines:

One of them is called cutthroat ruin. The other admits nothing through a fantasized gate.

ANNE HUTCHINSON

1591-1643

Asylum in Breath

I wanted to create a sanctuary, to enter the place where
the voice becomes servant of the voice.
So I must forego the old haven with its antithesis.

Humming there, the voice of space. As if it were
inside me. A caressing profanity.
And was I speechless in
the face of my unlearning.

The great cavity,
the air that surrounded the spire,
made a house of worship before my utterance,
a throat.

What they say a voice is: unauthorized as presence.
They say not to wage intimacy with this subject—
crooning, exaltation, inanity
　　　　　　as if an orphan would become its own sire.

No speaker speaks a foreign word with the
authority of a native tongue. But there

I hid, murmurous, handmaiden to my own attraction,
song whose pitch goes ever higher, ululating and
beguiled by fortifications from the unknown. Thus

a hymn becomes a ditty.
Beside it, this life is a continual interruption.

To hold a vowel in my very midst:
as hallowed consonants curtained off the word.

Still, the melody refuses to tire,
to pronounce the only other utterance for sanctuary. Chord of one tone prolonged.

Beloved Child

Your decease is as delicate as your birth. Unproven, like faith,
where both starting and ending are subject to change.

A hummingbird, russet and homely, moves past, eager
to suck the nectar from this place between:
the before and after.

                    The little creature is an angel of our curiosity
who wants to know how deep the well of sweetness will be
from this flower. Its wings hum so fast they are invisible,
always, like you, midway in flight.

                    That an angel could be so
plain, I wondered. That a spirit so small.
The density of waking besets us both, bird and mother,
from our misplaced chronologies.

I trust that you look on from your intermediate heaven.

Memory is your face. I touch the unsullied air
instead of it. Pain is the guardian that limits any trespass toward
you. I touch its air.

Lighter than that, the brown and mousy hummingbird hovers.
An angel, surely, with its insolence,
sinning against the loss of what a self is, unappeasably buoyant.

Anne Hutchinson and John Cotton

(How do grace and the law differ?)

Not by much,

not in the manner of our being able to

foresee

what is to come.

Go forward in the company

of such passion. Venture, as I did, clinging to a vision,

silent inside me. I prophesy the body shouldering its burden of knowledge:

always with its head bowed. The barest hesitation

becomes the soul's gratification. Reverence can read, in secret, this posture.

I hold fast. I did submit to grace. I traveled far. Many failed me, withheld

forgiveness, but I did confess myself.

There is no such authority

as the traveler's, the one lost in the wilderness, looking forward

to it and forbidden its foresight.

Anne Hutchinson on John Cotton

How do grace and the law differ? Not by much, he said,

not in the practice of faith that foretells how we will end. In his company,

others made such passage. The passion of his intelligence set sail, but rough

on the coast of his word.

To venture, as I did. I ventured to understand the vessel on which I sailed.

I hold a picture of it within me. To what source would the sojourner pray?

Waves ever break over the body with its head bowed. The barest hesitation

is the law's exile. None can say where this intelligence

came from. The soul endures by vexing itself and thus

it is ratified.

He said that I was free to strike from record the utterances I did not make. Yet

I make them as I made my infants inside me, seasick and clutched.

Grace travels far; its scrutiny is wanton. Many days it does not

forgive, nor will the tide repeat itself exactly. Burrowed within it, I was, perhaps, and did confess myself, the womb of another voice. There is no such figure of idolatry as birth, as the traveler's, the one lost in the ocean's wilderness, looking forward and forbidden all haven.

And Considering the Matter Again

(How do grace and the law differ?)

How does the law differ? he said,
Not in the cradle of our foreseeing.
We will end. We will chart the
custom of our limbs as they supplicate,
stretched upward.

Crossing, but rough,
on the coast of the body: this requires trust.
But to venture to understand, as I did,
faith unaligned
with trust. I formed the embryo of it
within me. I prayed my arms would be broken by the
storm overhead, and

the body bowed. Here lies the cradle
of exchange. He said. The barest contraction
makes birth into exile.
The soul's bliss endures by vexing itself.
He said that I was free to midwife the utterances I did not make. Yet
I make them as I made my infants, fresh and white.
The baby's scrutiny forsakes the womb
and clamors for the breast. Burrowed within it, I gave myself
suck. So he said. He said
there is no such figure of
idolatry as birth, except it be the haven of the breast.

Salvation

We measure vastness by the limit of our mortal life.

I would have you look, as example, at the face of the clock. It is a face, even as it cherishes its own absent mouth and closed eyes. Its example we should emulate.

See how it knows its cycle and yet repeats it daily. How the limit mimics the eternal. So this is salvation. With my closed eyes and shut mouth, I smell it. Here is the smell of the living upon us, dead in our clock of offense. We who endure and love our measure. My homily is my own perfume I breathe again and again. Paradise holds its enjoyments as repetition. Time is therefore pleasure as much as tedium. If my contradiction appears unholy, I have spoken my example well and timely.

If my Interlocutor were Faith

(Midwiving)

Can we have faith in the master who knows that the baby exists but cannot

coax it from the womb?

A cup cannot be enough evidence of its content.

There is another eye given to see the overflow,

          and a hand

that cradles the head as it is born from the gut of its mother, the hand

gladly stained with its birthing blood.

I have seen over and over one body given by another, enough

to know what faith is, like the water that cannot hold shape without

the curve of its cup,

          transparent.

Issuing forth from its exhausted mother. Too innocent. The formless baby.

If my Interlocutor were Grace

(Sewing and Spinning)

When the winter is treacherous and we are lost,

we do not grieve as we would prefer, but we

work.

Loss stitches the garments.

Fact is allegory of itself.

The yarn is spun at its own center and then knit together.

Dread grace

shows the willing hand its labor.

All the raveling, down to the smallest part,

furl and twist about,

is stubborn knowledge: its spirit as surely in the air

and the air also absent of parts.

If my Interlocutor were my Judge

I remind the scales that their undertaking is to balance,

and what one side holds, the other may differ from entirely,

only that their weight is the same.

Yet it is not so,

because the weight of difference itself is absolute,

averse to our appraisal.

What is damned in this measure, then, is assertion
where neither weight nor balance would stay it.

The mechanism beholds itself, preordained by its degree.
Unsteady.

Never was a tool so rightly insubordinate to the knowledge that would
claim it. Knowledge, not self-transcending, but mere measure.

The Language of the New World

That we, being explorers, abash the soil's cradle.

Discovering the baby as it babbles, overturned,
is our lullaby.
Our own darling, our own, our own,

shriven in the prattle of words, jabber, hush, coverlet, lips unearthing.

Soil's mantle we say, newborn words unmade for sense.

Embark

As I am. Now at sea. I feign sleep. I do
not sleep. Slush of water
slaps over the bowed sides of the ship. Stowaway. Why
then do I feel the woody
grain of the gangplank swinging
underfoot. As I embark. Sleeplessness is
the parody of departure. Who

goes nowhere finds rest.

Restlessness. The water's
counterpane upheaves itself.
Solaceless.

The stowaway awash, sleep-
less her tether to where
she wills herself and
will go.

Soothsaying

I would have perished had I

not believed

I would see a form of God

in the land of the living, the hand

of the living, a script

too crabbed to read,

and yet

the lines on God's palm

spread threefold

as roads on otherwise

untrod wilderness, lines as fortune

branched, stemming upward of my belief.

TWO PIRATES

1690-1782

Mary Reade

While I was captive,
I saw that horizon rhymes with reason.

And like so, the shape of the roof
beckons the hull of a boat.

It's the sun who decides, in the end,
whether the sea is a plateau or a well and how
such will clang on the atmosphere.

I was captive until I fell off the edge where the great heat
made me captain

of its lull and its whitecap.

I am mistress, now, of similarities.
My reason is to take and take now
as the horizon takes from me

or toward:

the bowed edges of a vessel never
secure or heal. The untoward advance

of light arrests

this surface as given.

Zig-zagging freedom to illumine
what I've wrested.

Reason rejects the curve.

Anne Bonney

When I looked forward
I was inclined to see

the point of convergence
wherein

all I valued lay,

and then
to see the same

piling up.

I never knew theft,
only domination;

as I was possessed,
so the possession

I bore from my body
and amid fight.

I am impatient with encounter,
just the fruit of it,

like a child dropped from my gut,
become an island.

Criminals forswear destination,
but my trove

is not embodied place
but the crosshairs

that endow its focus.

FERDINAND GREGOROVIUS

1821-1891

Gregorovius at Ninfa

1860

Perfection
is a kind

and here is its gate.

Why I hesitate
at the gate

rather than what surpasses it.

Inside it is O

and the circumnavigation
of the world

around the mouth
of the fountain.

That kind
which occurs by
nature is said

to gesture. The gesture
of the mouth

clasps the gate
from various location.

The spurt from
the interior.

Perfection of a kind
as to be

composed
of disarray.

This gesture returns
to the mouth

by way of wilderness.

Roundabout I would
beckon to the gate,

its shape in kind
a cup

dipped in.

Swelter and the perfect–
this garden–

circumspect to undo
what makes discovery

as to have been
the stave, the sound

before morning

as this representative
of a type.

Not known to exist in the dark,
then:

a victim

I went in to confess

the compass

who prevents the garden

from being implanted
with direction

I forget to circumlocute.

What kind
space cannot
circumvent.

THE CANUDOS REBELLION, BRAZIL

1893-1897

Sertaneja

You forfeit the landscape
by having hidden in it.

There is a poverty
that arises from skill.

Camouflaged in
vacancy, unbeatable.

            [These beliefs

            fall from the world's

            custody: You thought many things that
            were untrue. You thought
            the surface of the sun

            was comparatively
            less exposed.]

Your hand stings in its hiding place.

Destitute, your hand,
pointing at the comparison.

This shabby finger
on the last branch on the field
in final endlessness undeclared.

Follower

Once upon a time, she said,
shaving her head, there was
a girl of pure intention, and
I was she.

So high she lived,
and of such crude material
her habit

of abode.

It must be taken away.

And that is why, she ended,
I am here now. And I will always be

so intended
to this union. And there

the blade dropped

before which disclosure.

Why They Were Faithful

The product of the body

is nectar

and in this new and mystical science

we are true to follow

that nectar to the body

altered. We drink nectar

of the followers, and who

we ordain

to prod, to sigh in

new pain, adheres

to truth. One body,

making do. True drink

in this ordained truth.

The Broken Man of Natuba

What is real

deforms its witnesses.

Thus you:

the phenomenon following the phenomenon.

This procession.

You tear

a ray from the intolerant sun

and brandish,

you, with your shattered arms

and foreshortened legs.

Convection follows on

serration. What reality

does not include. This

noble deformity

called fact,

as it leads,

will famish the dirt track.

Memory

Being the wealthy ones—

eating coconut cake, having

coins stolen, having the world

behave as a white and porous skirt

that locks the room in shade.

Yes, set apart and watching

the shit fall to the mosaic

walkway, watching the leash

to the shit remain tranquil

in pattern.

The Unknown One

He holds his baffle

to the surrounding army.

He holds his family

between his neck and his

severed head.

Now the kindred swallow on his behalf.

When he has died,

he calls a translator to his side.

When he has died,

all of them return to their own proportion.

Heedful, the parts of the body

refuse their own concert,

invaders drinking.

Hungry

Did they lock

the empty building

or did this sojourner

open it with the

peculiar body of privation?

Walls are both sturdy and hollow.

The walls die eventually

in their migrations,

but bolstered by bowls,

cutlery, cups, and platters.

What cavities exist inside the pilgrim—

That typical weather sotters a follower to the ground.

Battle turned inside out

and spreading from station,

not shelter. The day's withering implements.

Sound at Night

What no one could lay

an ear on. What far distant

capital briefly

disturbed made cry

here. The steps

a child carves

at the base of a cathedral.

Din.

The cry of the trickle.

Now they steal the sound

from its final owner

who had so little else.

Report.

Someone sings

that a bath is being drawn

in this place long

since evaporated.

Riddle

And what will you do

when your papa finds you here?

I will smell the magic exhaust

that I emit when he beats me.

And what will you do

when your mama finds you here?

I will bring back a pure thing for her.

What will you do when the shopkeeper

wishes to weigh you on his scale?

I will give him his teeth, his plate,

and the condiments.

What will you do in the dark?

I will sing the overheard song,

the one who swerves tightly toward my own throat.

Disappearance

What we've shared in common

has made us sink.

The earth floor,

swept clean so many times,

clings to speech. Ubiquitous

sunlight

shows us these particles

as we dwindle beneath them.

Literally smaller than what

we spawn,

to see the voice

diffused in this matter.

Lack

If the lack can press onto

the body, and the wandering

body can return to its housing,

the back of the pressure

pushed through the door

can turn the house inside out,

then this body wonders less

what return is, where the turn is.

Something is gone

from the body. It needed

food's presentiment before

the pilgrim wandered away

from the turn of the compass,

the house lacking god, no door's

durability before its cavity

pressing on.

Nomad

Our place of departure

was all starvation,

but here

the sky's griddle

onto which we throw

fistfulls

of dust, such

piquant savor,

while we see

how our tread

nourishes the food
of gravity.

Learned wanderers

reject this rumor:

that the soil revolves

under firmament's

rolling heat.
What we know

is to have hunger inside
any revolution.

The Mermaid and her Fan

In response to a gift
she gave her own
and implored its repair.

The mermaid says,
"The world is white;
make it more white."
What gift
returns as breath
with each movement
of fin or hand

I gave slightlingly
as shore or
inhaled as
just foam
of possession

on the white

air

where it was breaking.

Folded Paper

Let the page be a cliff

over which some population

is shoved

and comes back to color the page

with its folds.

One day here, and the next not.

The paper stays

and marks what would have been the crease.

Stain is not ink

and the script will testify

only by its fine order.

Let disappearance be a remedy.

Harvest

In this story,

only those who have faces

can be grotesque.

Citizens of no memory

care nothing for size.

When we say "fit"

we mean that we know

the dimensions

are paltry.

Smaller, the figures

pieced onto the landscape.

Stitches,
meager on the shoddy blanket
of land.

This is the story

of a sequence:

consequence, loyalty, battle.

History prefers adherence.

The story acretes, warps, and opens

on the story

of what thing may

follow upon another:

it is not history

if history refuses the redundance

this spell

in time struggles to return.

2023

Legion

So opens another chapter of dust. Let's

agree to situate our shack here. We will

indeed make this commitment. Floods, earthquakes,

apocalyptic fires, and a determined training of our

vision on the last stand of pessimistic trees. We are here

together.

Here we decide to be one inside another and, imagine,

we will embark on new decimations, the sequencing of the millions

of the solitary us, the oxymoron of the plural, glib and less

glib as DNA, slow pulling apart of the parts

of flood, earthquake, conflagration, and this humble body

on body. So closes another chapter of dust, but this time

overpopulating our despair toward some kind of reversal. Were

we deciduous, were we transposed to our own horizon? We were

less decisive, atomized, made over and over of grim foresight and

fire. Floods, too, and the avalanche all accompanied us as plural. We
imagined a you who would come here, to us, a part of you, many parts,
insistence

upending despair, not taking it away. It too has many parts, too many
body on bodies. Relief, we decide, is one of our forms, a necessary
unclarity. Particle silted from particle. Here. We agree.
We will always disagree. Made of these parts, some of them
buried, but a chapter nonetheless. Here closes and opens the
horizon. Part pulled from part, we are an oxymoron. The
numerous horizon.